AL-ADHKAAR

Collection of Supplications and Glorifications from the Qur'an and Sunnah

Masjid Mubarak (NAIM), Newark, NJ

D1571093

Table of Contents

Foreword

This is a collection of adhkaar (supplications and words of glorification and remembrance) from the Qur'an, the Prophetic traditions (Sunnah), as well as some popular general prayers. It is our hope that this humble effort will benefit the Muslim community and anyone looking to gain the reward of supplications to Allah and to achieve the peace and tranquility that comes from engaging in contemplative remembrance of Allah and spiritual mindfulness. The audio recording of many of these adhkaar is available on our website at: **https://naimnj.org/audio/**

Finally, we remind ourselves and our brethren of the following admonitions of our beloved Prophet Muhammad (peace be upon him) concerning the importance of engaging in dhikr:

"Supplication is the essence of worship." - Sunan al-Tirmidhi

"The hearts are vessels and some have greater capacity than others. When you ask from Allah Almighty, O people, then ask Him while you are convinced He will answer. Verily, Allah does not answer the supplication of a servant from behind an unmindful heart." - Musnad Ahmad

"Keep your tongue moist with the remembrance of Allah." - Sunan al-Tirmidhi

"No people gather to remember Allah Almighty but that the angels surround them, cover them with mercy, send tranquility upon them, and mention them to Allah among those near to Him." - Sahih Muslim

Introduction

Following are a few tips about dhikr, which hopefully are helpful in ensuring that we derive optimum spiritual and moral benefits from our practice of it.

Literally, the Arabic word dhikr means the 'remembrance' or 'mention' of something. In the present context, it means the 'remembrance' of Allah through the mention of words of praise and glorification of Allah, words by which one seeks His forgiveness and assistance, and words by which one invokes His blessings for Prophet Muhammad (pbuh). Allah urges Muslims to do dhikr of Him constantly and promises a richly reward to those who do so (Qur'an 33:35,42).

Dhikr may be done individually or in congregation: Allah loves and rewards those who remember and praise Him whether individually or collectively (Hadith). Each of the five daily prayers involves a lot of dhikr not only following the end of, but even during the salat.

Dhikr does <u>not</u> consist in mere utterances if they are devoid of reflection on the message of what is being said. Dhikr must involve:
- *a profound sense of humility, as in the presence of Allah, during the dhikr;*
- *reflecting as deeply as possibly on what you are saying;*
- *resolving to live up to the message conveyed by the words uttered;*
- *lowering of the voice, and being alert and serious-minded as Allah has directed.*

May Allah illuminate our hearts through our dhikr and grant us full spiritual and material benefits thereof in the life of this world and richly rewards in the life to come.

Imam Nuruddeen M. Ali
Masjid Mubarak, Newark, NJ

Al-Adhkaar

اللّٰهُمَّ لَكَ الحَمْدُ أَنْتَ نُورُ السَّمَاوَاتِ وَالأَرْضِ وَمَنْ فِيهِنَّ، وَلَكَ الحَمْدُ أَنْتَ قَيِّمُ السَّمَاوَاتِ وَالأَرْضِ وَمَنْ فِيهِنَّ، وَلَكَ الحَمْدُ أَنْتَ رَبُّ السَّمَاوَاتِ وَالأَرْضِ وَمَنْ فِيهِنَّ

Allahumma lakal-hamdu Anta Noorus-samawaati wal-ardi wa man fihinna, wa lakal-hamdu Anta Qayyimus-samawaati wal-ardi wa man fihinna, wa lakal-hamdu Anta Rabbus-samawaati wal-ardi wa man fihinna.

O Allah! For You is all Praise - You are the Light of the Heavens and the Earth and all that is in them; and for You is all Praise – You are the Guardian of the Heavens and the Earth and all that is in them; and for You is all Praise – you are the Lord of the Heavens and the Earth and all that is in them.

فَسُبْحَٰنَ ٱللَّهِ حِينَ تُمْسُونَ وَحِينَ تُصْبِحُونَ ۝ وَلَهُ ٱلْحَمْدُ فِى ٱلسَّمَٰوَٰتِ وَٱلْأَرْضِ وَعَشِيًّا وَحِينَ تُظْهِرُونَ ۝ يُخْرِجُ ٱلْحَىَّ مِنَ ٱلْمَيِّتِ وَيُخْرِجُ ٱلْمَيِّتَ مِنَ ٱلْحَىِّ وَيُحْىِ ٱلْأَرْضَ بَعْدَ مَوْتِهَآ ۚ وَكَذَٰلِكَ تُخْرَجُونَ

Fasubhana Allahi heena tumsoona waheena tusbihoon.
Wa lahul hamdu fis samaawaati wal ardi wa 'ashiyyanw wa heena tuzhiroon. Yukhrijul haiya minal maiyiti wa yukhrijul maiyita minal haiyi wa yuhyil arda ba'da mawtihaa; wa kazaalika tukhrajoon.

So, glorify Allah in the evening and the morning. To Him is the praise in the Heavens and the Earth and in the last hours and when it is noon. He brings the living out of the dead and brings the dead out of the living and brings to life the earth after its lifelessness. And thus will you be brought out.

أَمْسَيْنَا وَأَمْسَى الْمُلْكُ لِلَّهِ رَبِّ الْعَالَمِينَ اللَّهُمَّ إِنِّي أَسْأَلُكَ خَيْرَ هَذِهِ اللَّيْلَةِ فَتْحَهَا وَنَصْرَهَا وَنُورَهَا وَبَرَكَتَهَا وَهُدَاهَا وَأَعُوذُ بِكَ مِنْ شَرِّ مَا فِيهَا وَشَرِّ مَا بَعْدَهَا

Amsaynaa wa amsal mulku lillah Rabbil alameen, Allahummah innee as aluka khayra aadhihi laylah, fathaha, wa nasraha, wa nuraha, wa barakataha, wa hudaha, wa audhu bika min sharri maa feeha wa sharri maa b`adaha
The evening has come to me and the whole universe belongs to Allah who is The Lord of the worlds. O Allah, I ask of you the good of the night, it's success and aid and its nur (celestial light) and barakaat (blessings) and seek hidayat (guidance) and refuge from the evil of this night and the evil that is to come later.

رَضِيتُ بِاللَّهِ رَبًّا وَبِالْإِسْلَامِ دِينًا وَبِمُحَمَّد نَبِيًّا

Raditu Billahi Rabban wa bil Islami Deenan wa bi Muhammadin Sallallahu Alayhi was-Sallama Nabiyyah
I am pleased with Allah as my Lord, Islam as my Deen (religion) and Muhammad (SAW) as my Nabi (prophet).

2

أَنْتَ الْحَقُّ وَوَعْدُكَ الْحَقُّ وَقَوْلُكَ الْحَقُّ وَلِقَاؤُكَ حَقٌّ وَالْجَنَّةُ حَقٌّ وَالنَّارُ حَقٌّ وَالسَّاعَةُ حَقٌّ وَالنَّبِيّونَ حَقٌّ وَمُحَمَّدٌ حَقٌّ

Antal-Haqqu wa wa'dukal-haqqu wa qawlukal-haqqu wa liqa'uka haqqun, wal-jannahtu haqqun wan-naru haqqun, was-sa'atu haqqun, wan-nabiyyoona haqqun wa Muhammadun haqq.

O Allah! You are the Truth, Your Promise is True, Your Speech is True, Your Meeting is True, Paradise is True, the Hellfire is True, the Hour is True, the Prophets are True, and Muhammad is True.

اللَّهُمَّ أَسْلَمْتُ نَفْسِي إِلَيْكَ، وَفَوَّضْتُ أَمْرِي إِلَيْكَ، وَوَجَّهْتُ وَجْهِي إِلَيْكَ، وَأَلْجَأْتُ ظَهْرِي إِلَيْكَ، رَغْبَةً وَرَهْبَةً إِلَيْكَ، لَا مَلْجَأَ وَلَا مَنْجَا مِنْكَ إِلَّا إِلَيْكَ، آمَنْتُ بِكِتَابِكَ الَّذِي أَنْزَلْتَ وَبِنَبِيِّكَ الَّذِي أَرْسَلْتَ

Allaahumma aslamtu nafsee ilayka, wa fawwadhtu amree ilayka, wa wajjahtu wajhee ilayka, wa alja'tu dhahree ilayka, raghbatan wa rahbatan ilayka, laa malja wa laa manja minka illaa ilayka, aamantu bikitaabikal-ladhee anzalta wa bi-nabiyyikal-ladhee arsalta.

O Allah, I submit myself to You, entrust my affairs to You, turn my face to You, and lay myself down depending upon You, hoping in You and fearing You . There is no refuge, and no escape, except to You. I believe in Your Book (the Qur'an) that You revealed, and the Prophet whom You sent.

اللهُمَّ صَلِّ عَلَى مُحَمَّدٍ وَعَلَى آلِ مُحَمَّدٍ كَمَا صَلَّيْتَ عَلَى إِبْرَاهِيمَ وَعَلَى آلِ إِبْرَاهِيمَ إِنَّكَ حَمِيدٌ مَجِيدٌ، وَبَارِكْ عَلَى مُحَمَّدٍ وَعَلَى آلِ مُحَمَّدٍ كَمَا بَارَكْتَ عَلَى إِبْرَاهِيمَ وَعَلَى آلِ إِبْرَاهِيمَ إِنَّكَ حَمِيدٌ مَجِيدٌ

Allahumma salli 'alaa Muhammadin wa 'alaa aali Muhammad, kamaa sallayta 'alaa Ibraheema wa 'alaa aali Ibrahim, Innaka hameedun Majeed. Wa barik 'alaa Muhammadin wa 'alaa aali Muhammad, kama barakta 'alaa Ibrahima wa 'alaa aali Ibrahim, Innaka hameedun majeed.

O Allah! Send prayers upon Muhammad and upon the followers of Muhammad, just as you sent prayers upon Ibrahim and upon the followers of Ibrahim. Verily, you are Praiseworthy, Glorious. And O Allah! Send blessings upon Muhammad and upon the followers of Muhammad, just as you sent blessings upon Ibrahim and upon the followers of Ibrahim. Verily, you are Praiseworthy, Glorious.

اللهُمَّ إِنَّا نَسْأَلُكَ بِأَنَّ لَكَ الحَمْدُ لا إِلهَ إِلا أَنْتَ، وَحْدَكَ لا شَرِيكَ لَكَ، المَنَّانُ، يَا بَدِيعَ السَّمَاوَاتِ وَالأَرْضِ، يَا ذَا الجَلالِ وَالإِكْرَامِ، يَا حَيُّ يَا قَيُّومُ.

Allahumma inna nas'aluka bi anna lakal-hamd, laa ilaha illa Ant, wahdaka la shareeka laka, Al-mannan, ya Badias-samawaati wal-ardi, ya Dhal-jalali wal-ikraam, ya Hayyu ya Qayyoom.

O Allah! We ask of You, by virtue of all praise being to You, there is no god worthy of worship but You alone, there is no partner for You, the Beneficent, Creator of the Heavens and the Earth, O Lord of Majesty and Bounty, O Alive Self-Subsisting One.

نَسْأَلُكَ بِأَنَّا نَشْهَدُ أَنَّكَ أَنْتَ اللهُ لا إِلهَ إِلا أَنْتَ، الأَحَدُ الصَّمَدُ الَّذِي لَمْ يَلِدْ وَلَمْ يُولَدْ وَلَمْ يَكُنْ لَهُ كُفُواً أَحَدْ

Nas'aluka bi ananaa nash-hadu annaka Antallah, la ilaha illa Ant, Al-ahadus-Samadu-ladhdhi lam yalid wa lam yu-lad wa lam yakul-lahu kufuwan ahad.

We ask You - by virtue of bearing witness that You are Allah, there is no god worthy of worship but You, the One, the Self-Sufficient, Who begets not, nor was He begotten, and there is none who is comparable to Him.

إِلَيْكَ نَشْكُو ضَعْفَ قُوَّتِنا وَقِلَّةَ حِيلَتِنا وَهَوَانَنا عَلَى النَّاسِ، يَا أَرْحَمَ الرَّاحِمِينَ، أَنْتَ رَبُّ الْمُسْتَضْعَفِينَ،

Ilayka nashku da'fa quwwatina, wa qillata heelatina, wa hawanana 'alan-naas, ya Arhamar-rahimeen. Anta rabbul-mustad'afeen
To You we complain of our weakness, our failure, our shame before the people. O Most Merciful! You are the Lord of the weak and oppressed.

وَأَنْتَ رَبُّنَا، إِلَى مَنْ تَكِلُنَا، إِلَى بَعِيدٍ يَتَجَهَّرُنَا، أَوْ إِلَى عَدُوٍّ مَلَّكْتَهُ أَمْرَنَا، إِنْ لَمْ يَكُنْ بِكَ غَضَبٌ عَلَيْنَا فَلا نُبَالِي، غَيْرَ أَنَّ عَافِيَتَكَ هِيَ أَوْسَعُ لَنَا

Wa Anta Rabbuna, ila man takiluna, ila ba'eedin yatajahharuna, aw ila 'aduwwin mallaktahu amrana, in lam yakun bika ghadabun 'alaynaa fala nubaali, ghayra anna 'afiyataka hiya awsa'u lana.
And You are our Lord, to whom will you entrust us? To a distant person who will treat us with enmity, or to an enemy You have made over us. If You are not angry at us, we would not care, for Your pardon is greater for us.

نَعُوذُ بِنُورِ وَجْهِكَ الَّذِي أَشْرَقَتْ لَهُ الظُّلُمَاتُ، وَصَلُحَ عَلَيْهِ أَمْرُ الدُّنْيَا وَالآخِرَةِ، أَنْ يَحِلَّ عَلَيْنَا غَضَبُكَ، وَأَنْ يَنْزِلَ بِنَا سَخَطُكَ، لَكَ الْعُتْبَى حَتَّى تَرْضَى، وَلا حَوْلَ وَلا قُوَّةَ إِلا بِكَ،

Na'udhu bi noori wajhikal-ladhi ashraqat lahudh-dhulumat, wa saluha 'alayhi amrud-dunya wal-akhirah, ay-yahilla alayna ghadabuk, wa ay-yanzila bina sakhatuk, lakal-'utbaa hatta tarda, wa la hawla wa la quwwata illa bik.

We seek refuge in the Light of Your Face for which darkness shine, and with which the affairs of this life and the Hereafter become good, from Your anger or displeasure fall upon us. You have the right to admonish until You are pleased, and there is no power and no might except in You.

لا إِلهَ إلاَ اللهُ العَظِيمُ الحَلِيم، لا إِلهَ إلا اللهُ رَبُّ العَرْشِ العَظِيمِ، لا إِلهَ إلا اللهُ رَبُّ السَّمَاوَتِ وَرَبُّ الأَرْضِ وَرَبُّ العَرْشِ الكَرِيم

La ilaha illAllahul Adhimul-Haleem. La ilaha illAllahu, Rabbul-arshil-adheem. La ilaha illAllahu Rabbus-samawaati wa Rabbul-ardi wa Rabbul-arshil-kareem.

There is no god worthy of worship but Allah, the Mighty the Forbearing, there is no god worthy of worship but Allah, Lord of the Mighty Throne, There is no god worthy of worship but Allah, Lord of the Heavens and Lord of the Earth and Lord of the Noble Throne

اللهُمَّ إِنَّا نَجْعَلُكَ في نُحُورِهِمْ، وَنَعُوذُ بِكَ مِنْ شُرُورِهِمْ،

Allahumma inna naj'aluka fi nuhoorihim, wa na'udhu bika min shuruurihim.

O Allah! We want Your help against them and seek Your protection against their atrocities.

رَبَّنَا، أَنْتَ عَضِيدُنَا، وَأَنْتَ نَصِيرُنَا، وَأَنْتَ حَسْبُنَا وَنِعْمَ الْوَكِيلِ

Rabbana Anta adeeduna wa Anta naseeruna, wa Anta hasbuna wa ni'mal-wakeel.

O Allah! You are our Helper, and You are our Victor, and You are Sufficient for us, and the Best Guardian.

لَا إِلهَ إِلا أَنْتَ سُبْحَانَكَ، إِنَّ كُنَّا مِنَ الظَّالِمِينَ

La ilaha illa Anta subhanaka, inna kunna minadh-dhalimeen.

There is not god worthy of worship but You, Glory be to You, truly we have been of the wrongdoers.

اللهُمَّ رَبَّنَا عَزَّ جَارُكَ، وَجَلَّ ثَنَاؤُكَ، وَتَقَدَّسَتْ أَسْمَاؤُكَ، اللهُمَّ لَا يُرَدُّ أَمْرُكَ وَلَا يُهْزَمُ جُنْدُكَ سُبْحَانَكَ وَبِحَمْدِكَ

Allahumma Rabbana azza jaaruk, wa jalla thana'uk, wa taqaddasat asma'uk, Allahumma la yuraddu amruk, wa la yuhzamu junduk, subhanaka wa bi hamdik

O Allah! Your allies are strong, Your praise is glorified, Your names are sanctified. O Allah! Your command cannot be repelled, and Your armies cannot be defeated.

اللهُمَّ لا تَجْعَلْ لِكَافِرٍ عَلَيْنَا سَبِيلاً، اللهُمَّ إِنَّا نَعُوذُ بِكَ مِنْ سُوءِ القَضَاءِ، وَدَرْكِ الشَّقَاءِ، وَشَمَاتَةِ الأَعْدَاءِ، وَجَهْدِ البَلاءِ، وَنَعُوذُ بِكَ مِنْ مُنْكَرَاتِ الأَخْلاقِ وَالأَعْمَالِ وَالأَهْوَاءِ وَالأَدْوَاءِ

Allahumma la taj'al li kafirin alayna sabeela, Allahumma inna na'udhu bika min suu'il-qada, wa darkish-shaqa', wa shamatatil-a'da', wa jahdil-bala', wa na'udhu bika min munkaratil-akhlaqi wal-amali wal-ahwa'i wal-adwa'
O Allah! Do not grant a disbeliever any way to harm us. O Allah! We seek refuge in You from a bad decree, being overtaken by misery, the gloats of the enemies, and the pains of afflictions, and we seek refuge in You from the disliked manners, deeds, desires, and diseases.

اللهُمَّ ارْفَعْ عَنَّا الغَلا وَالوَبَاءَ وَالرِّبا وَالزِّنا وَالزَّلازِلَ وَالمِحَنَ وَسُوءَ الفِتَنِ، مَا ظَهَرَ مِنْهَا وَما بَطَنَ

Allahummar-fa' 'annal-ghala wal-waba' war-riba waz-zina wal-zalazila wal-mihan, wa suu al-fitan, ma dhahara minha wa ma batan
O Allah! Remove from us transgression, plagues, usury, fornication, earthquakes and tests, and bad trials, both apparent and hidden...from this land of ours especially and from all lands of the Muslims, with Your Mercy, O Most Merciful!

اللَّهُمَّ اغْفِرْ لِي ذَنْبِي كُلَّهُ، دِقَّهُ وَجِلَّهُ، وَأَوَّلَهُ وَآخِرَهُ وَعَلَانِيَتَهُ وَسِرَّهُ

Allaahum-maghfir lee dhanbee kullahu, diqqahu wa jillahu, wa 'awwalahu wa 'aakhirahu wa 'alaaniyatahu wa sirrahu.
O Allah forgive me all my sins, great and small, the first and the last, those that are apparent and those that are hidden.

سُبْحَانَ ذِي الْجَبَرُوتِ، وَالْمَلَكُوتِ، وَالْكِبْرِيَاءِ، وَالْعَظَمَةِ

Subhaana thil-jabarooti, walmalakooti, walkibriyaa'i, wal'adhamati.
Glory is to You, Master of power, of dominion, of majesty and greatness.

سُبْحَانَ اللهِ وَبِحَمْدِهِ: عَدَدَ خَلْقِهِ، وَرِضَا نَفْسِهِ، وَزِنَةَ عَرْشِهِ وَمِدَادَ كَلِمَاتِهِ

Subhanallahi wa bihamdih: `adada khalqih, wa rida nafsih, wa zinata `arshih, wa midada kalimatih.
Glory is to Allah and praise is to Him, by the multitude of His creation, by His Pleasure, by the weight of His Throne, and by the extent of His Words.

اللَّهُمَّ إِنِّي أَسْأَلُكَ الْعَفْوَ وَالْعَافِيَةَ فِي الدُّنْيَا وَالْآخِرَةِ، اللَّهُمَّ إِنِّي أَسْأَلُكَ الْعَفْوَ وَالْعَافِيَةَ فِي دِينِي وَدُنْيَايَ وَأَهْلِي، وَمَالِي، اللَّهُمَّ اسْتُرْ عَوْرَاتِي، وَآمِنْ رَوْعَاتِي، اللَّهُمَّ احْفَظْنِي مِنْ بَيْنِ يَدَيَّ، وَمِنْ خَلْفِي، وَعَنْ يَمِينِي، وَعَنْ شِمَالِي، وَمِنْ فَوْقِي، وَأَعُوذُ بِعَظَمَتِكَ أَنْ أُغْتَالَ مِنْ تَحْتِي

Allaahumma innee as alukal 'afwa wal'aafiyata fid-dunyaa wal'aakhirah. Allaahumma innee as alukal afwa wal aafiyata fee deenee wa dunyaaya wa ahlee, wa maalee. Allaahummastur 'awraatee, wa 'aamin raw'aatee. Allaahummah fadhnee min bayni yadayya, wa min khalfee, wa an yameenee, wa an shimaalee, wa min fawqee, wa 'a'oodhu bi 'adhamatika 'an 'ughtaala min tahtee.
O Allah, I seek Your forgiveness and Your protection in this world and the next. O Allah, I seek Your forgiveness and Your protection in my religion, in my worldly affairs, in my family and in my wealth. O Allah, conceal my

secrets and preserve me from anguish. O Allah, guard me from what is in front of me and behind me, from my left , and from my right , and from above me . I seek refuge in Your Greatness from being struck down.

اللّٰهُمَّ إِنِّي أَسْأَلُكَ يا اللهُ بِأَنَّكَ الواحِدُ الأَحَد الصَّمَدُ الَّذي لَمْ يَلِدْ وَلَمْ يولَدْ،وَلَمْ يَكنْ لَهُ كُفُواً أَحَد ،أَنْ تَغْفِرْ لي ذُنوبي إِنَّكَ أَنْتَ الغَفورُ الرَّحِيم

Allahhumma inni as'aluka Ya Allahu bi annakal-Wahidul Ahadu Samadul ladhi, lam ya-lid wa lam-youlad, wa lam yakullahu kufwan Ahad, an taghfira-li dhunuubi innaka Antal-Ghafoorur-Raheem
Oh Allah, I ask, Oh Allah, You are the One, The Only, Self-Sufficient Master, Who was not Begotten and Begets not, And none is equal to Him, Forgive me my sins, surely You are Forgiving, Merciful.

اللَّهُمَّ عَافِني في بَدَني اللَّهُمَّ عَافِني في سَمْعي اللَّهُمَّ عَافِني في بَصَري لَا إِلَهَ إِلَّا أَنْتَ

Allahumma 'aafini fi badani, Allahumma 'aafini fi sam'i, Allahumma 'aafini bi basari La illaha ila Anta
O Allah! Grant me health in my body. O Allah! Grant me good hearing. O Allah! Grant me good eyesight. There is no god worthy of worship but You.

اللّهُمَّ أَنْتَ رَبِّي لا إلهَ إلاَّ أَنْتَ خَلَقْتَني وَأَنا عَبْدُكَ وَأَنا عَلى عَهْدِكَ وَوَعْدِكَ
ما اسْتَطَعْت أَعوذُ بِكَ مِنْ شَرِّ ما صَنَعْت أَبوءُ لَكَ بِنِعْمَتِكَ عَلَيَّ وَأَبوءُ
بِذَنْبي فَاغْفِرْ لي فَإِنَّهُ لا يَغْفِرُ الذُّنوبَ إلاَّ أَنْتَ

Allahumma Anta Rabbi, La ilaha illa Anta, Khlaqtani Wa Ana Abduka, wa ana alaa `adika wa w'a dika mastatatu. Ahudhu bika min Sharri ma san`atu, Abuuhu laka bi ni`imatika alayya wa abuuhu bidhanbi Fagfir lee fainnahu la yagfiru dhunuba illaa Anta.

Oh Allah, You are my Lord, there is none worthy of worship but You. You created me and I'm your servant. I keep Your covenant, and my pledge to You so far as I am able. I seek refuge in You from the evil of what I have done. I admit to Your blessings upon me, and I admit to my misdeeds. Forgive me for there is none who may forgive sins but You.

اللهُمَّ يَا حَيُّ يَا قَيُّومُ بِرَحْمَتِكَ نَسْتَغِيثُ، أَصْلِحْ لَنَا شَأْنَنَا كُلَّهُ، وَلا تَكِلْنَا إلى
أَنْفُسِنَا طَرْفَةَ عَيْنٍ ولا أَقَلَّ مِنْ ذَلِكَ

Allahumma Ya Hayyu Ya Qayyoom, bi rahmatika nastagheeth, aslih lana sha'nana kullahu wa la takilna ila anfusina tarfata aynin wa la aqalla min dhalik.

O Ever-Living! O Self-Subsisting! and Supporter of all! By Your Mercy we seek assistance, rectify for us all our affairs and do not leave us to ourselves even for the blink of an eye or less than that.

اللَّهُ أَكْبَرُ، اللَّهُ أَعَزُّ مِنْ خَلْقِهِ جَمِيعًا، اللَّهُ أَعَزُّ مِمَّا أَخَافُ وَأَحْذَرُ، وَأَعُوذُ بِاللَّهِ
الَّذِي لاَ إِلَهَ إِلاَّ هُوَ، الْمُمْسِكُ السَّمَاوَاتِ السَّبْعَ أَنْ يَقَعْنَ عَلَى الأَرْضِ إِلاَّ

بِإِذْنِهِ، مِنْ شَرِّ عَبْدِكَ، وَجُنُودِهِ وَأَتْبَاعِهِ وَأَشْيَاعِهِ مِنَ الْجِنِّ وَالإِنْسِ، اللَّهُمَّ كُنْ لِي جَارًا مِنْ شَرِّهِمْ، جَلَّ ثَنَاؤُكَ، وَعَزَّ جَارُكَ، وَتَبَارَكَ اسْمُكَ، وَلاَ إِلَهَ غَيْرُكَ

Allahu Akbar, Allahu a'azzu min khalqihi jammii'an. Allahu a'azzu mimma akhaafu wa ahdharu, wa a'udhu billahil-ladhi la illaha illa Huwa, al-Mumsik is-samaawaatis sab'i an yaqa'na alal-ardhi illa bi'idhnihi, min sharri 'abdika [name of the adversary], wa junoodihi wa atbaa'ihi wa ashaa'ihi, minal-jinni wal-insi. Allahumma kun li jaaran min sharrihim, jalla thanaa'uka wa 'azza jaarruka, wa tabaaraka-smuka, wa laa illaha ghairuka.

Allah is greater. Allah is mightier than all His creation and Allah is greater than all that is feared and all that you are wary of. I seek refuge with Allah. There is no god but Him, the One who keeps the seven heavens from falling onto the earth by nothing except His permission, from the evil of your slave {name of the adversary} and his armies and followers and supporters, both among jinn and men. O Allah, be my protector against their evil. Your praise is great, and Your protection is immense, Blessed is Your Name. There is no god but You (three times).

اَللَّهُمَّ أَصْلِحْ لِي دِينِي الَّذِي هُوَ عِصْمَةُ أَمْرِي, وَأَصْلِحْ لِي دُنْيَايَ الَّتِي فِيهَا مَعَاشِي, وَأَصْلِحْ لِي آخِرَتِي الَّتِي إِلَيْهَا مَعَادِي, وَاجْعَلِ الْحَيَاةَ زِيَادَةً لِي فِي كُلِّ خَيْرٍ, وَاجْعَلِ الْمَوْتَ رَاحَةً لِي مِنْ كُلِّ شَرٍّ

Allahumma aslih li diiniyalladhi huwa 'ismatu amri, wa aslih li dunyaya llati fiha ma'ashi; wa aslih li akhirati- llati ilaiha ma'aadi, waj'alil hayata ziyadatan li fi kulli khairin, waj'alil mawta rahatan li min kulli sharrin

O Allah! Set right for me my religion, which is the safeguard of my affairs. And set right for me the affairs of the world wherein is my living. Decree the Hereafter to be good for me. And make this life, for me, (a source) of abundance for every good and make my death (a source) of comfort to me and protection against every evil.

اللّٰهُمَّ إِنِّي عَبْدُكَ ابْنُ عَبْدِكَ ابْنُ أَمَتِكَ نَاصِيَتِي بِيَدِكَ مَاضٍ فِيَّ حُكْمُكَ عَدْلٌ فِيَّ قَضَاؤُكَ

أَسْأَلُكَ بِكُلِّ اسْمٍ هُوَ لَكَ سَمَّيْتَ بِهِ نَفْسَكَ أِوْ أَنْزَلْتَهُ فِي كِتَابِكَ أَوْ عَلَّمْتَهُ أَحَداً مِنْ خَلْقِكَ

أَوِ اسْتَأْثَرْتَ بِهِ فِي عِلْمِ الْغَيْبِ عِنْدَكَ أَنْ تَجْعَلَ الْقُرْآنَ رَبِيعَ قَلْبِي وَنورَ صَدْرِي وجَلَاءَ حُزْنِي وذَهَابَ هَمِّي

Allahumma inni 'abduka, ibnu 'abdika, ibnu amatika, naasiyati biyadika, maadhin fiyya hukumuka, 'adhlun fiyya qadha'uka as-aluka bi kulli ismin huwa laka, sammaita bihi nafsaka, aw an-zaltahu fi kitabika, aw 'allamtahu ahadan min khalqika, awista'tharta bihi fi 'ilmil-ghaibi 'indaka, an taj'alal-Qur'ana Rabbi'a qalbi, wa nura sadri, wa jalaa'a huzni, wa dhahaaba hammi

O Allah, I am Your servant, son of Your servant, son of Your maidservant, my forelock is in Your hand, Your command over me is forever executed and Your decree over me is just. I ask You by every name belonging to You which You named Yourself with, or revealed in Your Book, or You taught to any of Your creation, or You have preserved in the knowledge of the unseen with You, that You make the Qur'an the life of my heart and the light of my breast, and a departure for my sorrow and a release of my anxiety.

13

اللَّهُمَّ إِنِّي أَسْأَلُكَ خَيْرَ الْمَسْأَلَةِ، وَخَيْرَ الدُّعَاءِ، وَخَيْرَ النَّجَاحِ، وَخَيْرَ الْعِلْمِ، وَخَيْرَ الْعَمَلِ وَخَيْرَ الثَّوَابِ، وَخَيْرَ الْحَيَاةِ وَخَيْرَ الْمَمَاتِ، وَثَبِّتْنِي وَثَقِّلْ مَوَازِينِي، وَحَقِّقْ إِيمَانِي، وَارْفَعْ دَرَجَتِي، وَتَقَبَّلْ صَلَاتِي، وَاغْفِرْ خَطِيئَاتِي، وَأَسْأَلُكَ الْعُلَا مِنَ الْجَنَّةِ

Allahumma inni as'aluka khairal masalati, wa khairad-du'aai, wa khairan-najahi, wa khairal-'ilm wa khairal-'amali, wa khairath-thawabi, wa khairal-hayaati, wa khairal mamaati, wa thabbitni wa thaqqil mawaazini, wa haqqiq imaani warf'a darajati wa taqabbal salaati, wagfir khatiatii, wa as-alukalal-'ula minal-Jannah

Allah! I ask You for the Best affair, the Best supplication, the best success, Knowledge, the best deed, the best reward, the best life, and the best death. Keep me upright, make my Scale heavy, confirm my faith, raise high my status, accept my prayer, and forgive my sins. I ask You for high positions in Paradise.

اللَّهُمَّ اسْتُرْ عَوْرَتِي، وَآمِنْ رَوْعَتِي

Allahummastur 'auraati, wa aamin raw 'aati

O Allah! Cover up my defects, and change my fear into peace.

اللَّهُمَّ أَحْسِنْ عَاقِبَتَنَا فِي الأُمُورِ كُلِّهَا ، وَ أَجِرْنَا مِنْ خِزْيِ الدُّنْيَا وَ عَذَابِ الآخِرَةِ

Allahumma ahsin 'aqiba-tana fil-umuri kulliha, wa ajirna min khiz yiddunya wa adhabil Akhirah

14

O Allah! Make the result of all our affairs good, and deliver us from the disgrace of this world and the torment of the Hereafter.

أَعُوذُ بِكَلِمَاتِ اللّهِ التَّامَّاتِ مِنْ شَرِّ مَا خَلَقَ

Audhu bi kalimatillahit- taammati min sharri ma khalaqa
I seek refuge in the perfect words of Allah from the evil of what He has created.

Laa ilaha illa Allah, Laailaha illa Allah, Laailaha illa Allah, Antal-lahu, Allah, Allah
Anta Rabbi, Allah Allah; Anta Hasbee, Allah, Allah;
Antash-shaafi, Allah, Allah; Anta Kaafi, Allah, Allah.

Allahu, Ar-Rahmaanu,	**Laa ilaha illa Allah**
Ar-Rahimul Malikul Quddusu	**Laa ilaha illa Allah**
As-Salamul Mu`minul Muhayminu	**Laa ilaha illa Allah**
Al-'Azeezu Al-jabbaru	**Laa ilaha illa Allah**
Al-Mutakabbiru Al-khaliqu	**Laa ilaha illa Allah**
Al-Bariu Al-Musawwiru	**Laa ilaha illa Allah**
Al-Gaffaru Al-Wahhab	**Laa ilaha illa Allah**
Ar-Razzaku Al-Fattahu	**Laa Ilaha illa Allah**
Al-Alimul Qabidul Basitu	**Laa Ilaha illa Allah**
Al-Khafidu Ar-Rafiu	**Laa Ilaha illa Allah**
Al Mu'izzu Al Mudhillu	**Laa Ilaha illa Allah**
As-Samee'u Al-Baseeru	**Laa Ilaha illa Allah**
Al-Lateefu Al-Khabeeru	**Laa Ilaha illa Allah**
Al-Haleemu Al-'Azeemu	**Laa Ilaha illa Allah**
Al-Ghafuru As-Shakooru	**Laa Ilaha illa Allah**
Al-'Aliyyu Al-Kabeeru	**Laa Ilaha illa Allah**
Al-Hafeezu Al-Muqeetu	**Laa Ilaha illa Allah**
Al-Haseebu Al-Jaleelu	**Laa Ilaha illa Allah**
Al-Kareemu Ar-Roqibu	**Laa Ilaha illa Allah**
Al-Mujeebu Al-Wasiu	**Laa Ilaha illa Allah**
Al-Hakeemu Al-Wadoodu	**Laa Ilaha illa Allah**
Al-Majeedu Al-Bah'ithu	**Laa Ilaha illa Allah**
As-Shahidu Haqqul Wakeel	**Laa Ilaha illa Allah**
Al-Qawiyyu Al-Mateenu	**Laa Ilaha illa Allah**
Al-Waliyyu Al-Hameedu	**Laa Ilaha illa Allah**
Al-Muhseel Mubdiu	**Laa Ilaha illa Allah**
Al-Mu'eedul Muhyee	**Laa Ilaha illa Allah**
Al-Mumeetul Hayyu	**Laa Ilaha illa Allah**

Al-Qayyumu Al-Waajidu	Laa Ilaha illa Allah
Al-Maajidu Al-Wahidu	Laa Ilaha illa Allah
Al-Waahidu As-Somadu	Laa Ilaha illa Allah
Al-Qadiru Al-Muqtadiru	Laa Ilaha illa Allah
Al-Muqaddimul Muaakhiru	Laa Ilaha illa Allah
Al-Awwalu Al-Aakhiru	Laa Ilaha illa Allah
Az-Zaahiru Al-Baatinu	Laa Ilaha illa Allah
Al-Waaliee Al-Muta a`alee	Laa Ilaha illa Allah
Al-Barru At-Tawwabu	Laa Ilaha illa Allah
Al-Muntaqimu Al-'Afuwwu	Laa Ilaha illa Allah
Ar-Rauf Malikul Mulki	Laa Ilaha illa Allah
Dhul Jallali Wal ikram	Laa Ilaha illa Allah
Al-Muqsitu Al-Jaamiu	Laa Ilaha illa Allah
Al-Ghaniyyul Mughni	Laa Ilaha illa Allah
Al-Mani'u Ad-Darru	Laa Ilaha illa Allah
An-Naafiu An-Nuru	Laa Ilaha illa Allah
Al-Haadi Badee`u	Laa Ilaha illa Allah
Al-Baqi Al-Waarithu	Laa Ilaha illa Allah
Ar-Rasheed As-Sabooru	Laa Ilaha illa Allah
Inna Asmaakal 'Ulaa	Laa Ilaha illa Allah
Man Asaha Faqadnajaa	Laa Ilaha illa Allah
Fah-atina Khayra maabihaa	Laa Ilaha illa Allah
Robbi yassir Humooranaa	Laa Ilaha illa Allah
Latu`as-sir ilaahanaa	Laa Ilaha illa Allah
Fa 'afu'anna Wagfirlanaa	Laa Ilaha illa Allah
Thum-Marhamna Allah	Laa Ilaha illa Allah
Anta Ilahu ilaahanaa	Laa Ilaha illa Allah
Laatakilnaa li Amrinaa	Laa Ilaha illa Allah
Farham Kulla Aalina	Laa Ilaha illa Allah
Wahtinaa minka Rahmatan	Laa Ilaha illa Allah
Fid-Duna Thumma Walgadin	Laa Ilaha illa Allah
Laa ilaha illa Allah	Laa Ilaha illa Allah
Muhammadun Rasulullah	Laa Ilaha illa Allah

وَكَفَى بِاللّٰهِ وَلِيّاً وَكَفَى بِاللّٰهِ نَصِيراً

Wa kafa bi llahi waliyyan   **Wa kafa bi llahi naseera.**

And Allah suffices as a protector; and Allah suffices as helper.

Allah Allah Rabbunaa   **Allah Allah Hasbuna**

يَا كَرِيمُ هَبْ لِي * مَعْ جَفَاءٍ جَهْلِي

Yaa Karimu Hablee   **Ma`a Jafaahi Jahlee**
Oh Generous Allah! Forgive me those sins committed out my folly ignorance.

كَمْ رَجَاكَ مِثْلِي * لَمْ تُخِبْ رَجَاهُ

Kam Rajaaka Mithliya   **Lam Tukhib Raajahu**
You have forgiven uncountable souls that have been in this position before, Oh Allah grant my own request.

Allah Allah Rabbunaa   **Allah Allah Hasbuna**

خَالِقَ الْبَرَايَا * وَاهِبَ الْعَطَايَا

Khaliqal Baraaya   **Wahibal Ataya**
Oh Allah you are the creator and giver of bounteous gifts

دَافِعَ الْمَصَائِبِ * فَاسْتَجِبْ دُعَائِ

Daafial Masahibi   **Fastajib Dua`hi**

Oh Allah you are the protector against all evils please protect me and accept my prayer.

Allah Allah Rabbunaa   **Allah Allah Hasbuna**

أَنْتَ ذُو الْكَمَالِ * أَنْتَ ذُو الْجَلَالِ

Anta Dhul Jalali   **Anta Dhul Kamali**

Oh Your majesty, defectless, perfect and pure Allah!

أَنْتَ ذُو الْفَضَائِلِ * أَنْتَ ذُو النَّوَالِ

Anta Dhul Fadaili   **Anta Dhun-Nawali**

Oh Allah, You are virtuous and forgiver of all sins!

Allah Allah Rabbunaa   **Allah Allah Hasbuna**

أَنْتَ مَنْ تَرَانِي * تَسْمَعُ كَلَامِي

Anta Mantaraani   **Tasmau Kalami**

Oh Allah, You are the seer that sees me and listener who hears me.

تَعْلَمُ مَكَانِي * ثُمَّ لَا تَنْسَانِي

Ta`alamu Makaniya   **Thummah Laa Tansani**
Oh Allah, You know my situation and I am sure you will never forget me.

Allah Allah Rabbunaa   **Allah Allah Hasbuna**

اُسْتُرِ الْعُيُوبَ * اِغْفِرِ الذُّنُوبَ

Usturil Uyuba   **Igfir dhunuba**
Oh Allah, overlook my mistakes and forgive my sins.

لَا تُؤَاخِذَنِّي * فَضْلاً مِنْكَ رَبِّي

Laa Tuaakhidhanni   **Fadlan Minka Rabbee**
Oh Allah, do not punish me for what my hands have wrought and grant this as a special mercy from you.

اِرْحَمِ الْفَقِيرَ * اُجْبُرِ الْكَسِيرَ

Irhamil Faqira Allah   **Ijbiril Kasira, Allah**
Oh Allah show mercy on the less fortunate ones.

أَطْلِقِ الْأَسِيرَ * لُطْفًا يَا مُجِيبَ الدَّاعِي

Atliqil `Asira Lutfan   **Yaa Mujeebad-Dahi, Allah**
Oh Allah, free the captives as special compassion from you, because you are answerer of all prayers.

20

Allah Allah Rabbunaa   **Allah Allah Hasbuna**

أَوْصِلِ السَّلاَمَ * لِأَهْلِ الــسَّلاَمِ

Awsilis-Salaama Allah   **Li Ahlis-Salaami, Allah**

Oh Allah, continue to shower your mercies on those you have granted your mercy.

بِـدَارِ السَّـلاَمِ * تَحِيَّةً وَ سَلاَمَا

Bidaris-Salaami   **Tahiyyatan Was-Salaama, Allah**

Allah Allah Rabbunaa   **Allah Allah Hasbuna**

سُبْحَانَكَ رَبَّ الْعِزَّةِ * عَمَّا يَصِفُونَ بِصِفَةِ

Subhanaka Rabbil `Izzati**          **`Amma Yasifuna Bisifati

وَأَتَــمَّ اللهُ جَلاَلَهُ * اَللهُ جَـلَّ جَلاَلُهُ

Wa Atammallahu Jalalahu   **Allahu Jallah Jalaluhu**

حَمْدًا لِـحَيٍّ دَائِمٍ * شُكْرًا لِرَبِّي الْأَوْحَدِ

Hamdan Lihayyid-Daimi   **Shukran Lirabbil Awhadi**

صلُّوا على شَفِيعِنا* خيرِ المخلوقِ محمد

21

Salluu 'ala Shafee`ina   **Khayril Makhluki Muhammadi**

$$\text{سُبْحَانَكَ رَبَّ الْعِزَّةِ * عَمَّا يَصِفُونَ بِصِفَةِ}$$

Subhanaka Rabbil `Izzati**         **`Amma Yasifuna Bisifati

$$\text{وَأَتَمَّ اللهُ جَلَالَهُ * اَللهُ جَلَّ جَلَالُهُ}$$

Wa Atammallahu Jalalahu   **Allahu Jallah Jalaluhu**

$$\text{وَمِنْ كُلِّ مَا نَشْكُوهُ يَا رَبِّ عَافِنَا}$$

Wa Min Kulli Maa naskuhu Yaa rabbi aafinaa
O Allah, answer every call regarding that which I cry to You

$$\text{كَأَيُّوبَ إِذْ نَجَّيْتَهُ بَعْدَ بَلْوَاهُ}$$

Ka ayyuba idhi najjaytahu ba`ada balwaahu
As you did answer the prayer of prophet Ayyub when he called upon You

$$\text{اللهُ لَا إِلَهَ إِلَّا هُوَ الْحَيُّ الْقَيُّومُ لَا تَأْخُذُهُ سِنَةٌ وَلَا نَوْمٌ لَهُ مَا فِي}$$
$$\text{السَّمَاوَاتِ وَمَا فِي الْأَرْضِ مَنْ ذَا الَّذِي يَشْفَعُ عِنْدَهُ إِلَّا بِإِذْنِهِ يَعْلَمُ مَا بَيْنَ}$$
$$\text{أَيْدِيهِمْ وَمَا خَلْفَهُمْ وَلَا يُحِيطُونَ بِشَيْءٍ مِنْ عِلْمِهِ إِلَّا بِمَا شَاءَ وَسِعَ كُرْسِيُّهُ}$$
$$\text{السَّمَاوَاتِ وَالْأَرْضَ وَلَا يَئُودُهُ حِفْظُهُمَا وَهُوَ الْعَلِيُّ الْعَظِيمُ}$$

Allaahu laa ilaaha illaa Huwal-Hayyul-Qayyoom. Laa ta'khudhuhu sinatun wa laa nawm, lahu maa fis-samaawaati wa maafil-'ard. Man dhal-ladhee yashfa'u 'indahu 'illaa bi'idhnih. Ya'lamu maa bayna 'aydeehim wa maa khalfahum, wa laa yuheetoona bishay'in min 'ilmihi 'illaa bimaa shaa'a. Wasi'a kursiyyuhus-samaawaati wal'ardh, wa laa ya'ooduhu hifdhuhumaa, wa Huwal-'Aliyyul- 'Adheem.

Allah! There is none worthy of worship but He, the Ever Living, the One Who sustains and protects all that exists. Neither slumber nor sleep overtakes Him. To Him belongs whatever is in the heavens and whatever is on the earth. Who is he that can intercede with Him except with His Permission? He knows what happens to them in this world, and what will happen to them in the Hereafter. And they will never encompass anything of His Knowledge except that which He wills. His Throne extends over the heavens and the earth, and He feels no fatigue in guarding and preserving them. And He is the Most High, the Most Great.

رَبَّنَا رَبَّ الْخَلاَئِقِ * رَبَّنَا رَبَّ الْخَلاَئِقِ

Rabbanaa Rabbal Khalaaiqi
Our Lord! The lord of creations

Rabbanaa Rabbal Khalaaiqi
Our Lord! The lord of creations.

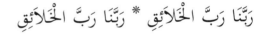

ن ۞ جِّنَا مِنْ شَرِّ الزَّمَانِ

Najjinaa Min Sharriz-Zamaani
Grant us refuge from problems, tribulations and calamity.

وَآتِنَا مِنْكَ السَّعَادَةَ * وَآتِنَا مِنْكَ السَّلاَمَةَ

23

Wa`atinaa Minkas-Sa`adata Wa`atina Minkas-Salamta
Grant us success from yourself   And   grant   us   peace   from
yourself.

وَالرِّضَا مَعْ نَيْلِ الْأَمَانِي

War rida ma`an naylil amaani
Also grant us Your pleasure and the achievement of our desires.

اللّهُمَّ آمِيــــن

Allahumma Ameen

O Allah! Please accept.

End of Adhkaar

Selected Special Prayers

Istikhaarah (Seeking Allah's Counsel)

Jabir bin Abdullah (RA) said: The Prophet (SAW) used to teach us to seek Allah's Counsel in all matters, as he used to teach us a Surah from the Qur'an. He would say: When anyone of you has an important matter to decide, let him pray two Rak'ahs other than the obligatory prayer, and then say:

اللَّهُمَّ إِنِّي أَسْتَخِيرُكَ بِعِلْمِكَ، وَأَسْتَقْدِرُكَ بِقُدْرَتِكَ، وَأَسْأَلُكَ مِنْ فَضْلِكَ الْعَظِيمِ، فَإِنَّكَ تَقْدِرُ وَلَا أَقْدِرُ، وَتَعْلَمُ، وَلَا أَعْلَمُ، وَأَنْتَ عَلَّامُ الْغُيُوبِ، اللَّهُمَّ إِنْ كُنْتَ تَعْلَمُ أَنَّ هَذَا الْأَمْرَ – خَيْرٌ لِي فِي دِينِي وَمَعَاشِي وَعَاقِبَةِ أَمْرِي – عَاجِلِهِ وَآجِلِهِ – فَاقْدُرْهُ لِي وَيَسِّرْهُ لِي ثُمَّ بَارِكْ لِي فِيهِ، وَإِنْ كُنْتَ تَعْلَمُ أَنَّ هَذَا الْأَمْرَ شَرٌّ لِي فِي دِينِي وَمَعَاشِي وَعَاقِبَةِ أَمْرِي – عَاجِلِهِ وَآجِلِهِ – فَاصْرِفْهُ عَنِّي وَاصْرِفْنِي عَنْهُ وَاقْدُرْ لِيَ الْخَيْرَ حَيْثُ كَانَ ثُمَّ أَرْضِنِي بِهِ

Allaahumma 'innee 'astakheeruka bi'ilmika, wa 'astaqdiruka biqudratika, wa as aluka min fadhlikal-'Adheemi, fa'innaka taqdiru wa laa 'aqdiru, wa ta'lamu, wa laa 'a'lamu, wa 'Anta 'Allaamul-Ghuyoobi, Allaahumma 'in kunta ta'lamu 'anna haadhal amra-(then mention the thing to be decided) Khayrun lee fee deenee wa ma'aashee wa 'aaqibati 'amree - (or say) 'Aajilihi wa 'aajilihi - Faqdurhu lee wa yassirhu lee thumma baarik lee feehi. Wa 'in kunta ta'lamu 'anna haadhal-'amra sharrun lee fee deenee wa ma'aashee wa 'aaqibati 'amree - (or say) 'Aajilihi wa 'aajilihi - Fasrifhu

'annee wasrifnee 'anhu waqdur liyal-khayra haythu kaana thummar dinee bihi.

O Allah, I seek the counsel of Your Knowledge, and I seek the help of Your Omnipotence, and I beseech You for Your Magnificent Grace. Surely, You are Capable and I am not. You know and I know not, and You are the Knower of the unseen. O Allah, if You know that this matter [then mention the thing to be decided] is good for me in my religion and in my life and for my welfare in the life to come, - [or say: in this life and the afterlife] - then ordain it for me and make it easy for me, then bless me in it. And if You know that this matter is bad for me in my religion and in my life and for my welfare in the life to come, - [or say: in this life and the afterlife] - then distance it from me, and distance me from it, and ordain for me what is good wherever it may be, and help me to be content with it.

Dear brethren, know that whoever seeks the counsel of the Creator will not regret it and whoever seeks the advice of the believers will feel confident about his decisions. Allah says in the Qur'an: "*And consult them in the affair. Then when you have taken a decision, put your trust in Allah.*" - Al-Imran 3:159

Morning Supplication

أَصْبَحْنا وَأَصْبَحَ المُلكُ للهِ رَبِّ العالَمين ، اللّهُمَّ إِنِّي أَسْأَلُكَ خَيْرَ هذا اليَوْمِ، فَتْحَهُ ، وَنَصْرَهُ ، وَنورَهُ وَبَرَكَتَهُ ، وَهُداهُ ، وَأَعوذُ بِكَ مِنْ شَرِّ ما فيهِ وَشَرِّ ما بَعْدَه

Asbahana wa asbahal mulku lillah rabbil alameen, Allahummah innee as aluka khayra aadhal yawmi, fathahu, wa nasrahu, wa nurahu, wa barakatahu, wa hudahu, wa audhu bika min sharri maa feehi wa sharri maa b`adahu.

26

The morning has come to me and the whole universe belongs to Allah, the Lord of the worlds, O Allah, I ask of you the good of the day, it's success and aid and it's nur (celestial light) and barakaat (blessings) and seek hidayah (guidance) and seek refuge from the evil in it (this day) and from the evil of that which is to come later.

Evening Supplication

أَمْسَيْنَا وَأَمْسَى الْمُلْكُ لِلَّهِ رَبِّ الْعَالَمِينَ اللَّهُمَّ إِنِّي أَسْأَلُكَ خَيْرَ هَذِهِ اللَّيْلَةَ فَتْحَهَا وَنَصْرَهَا وَنُورَهَا وَبَرَكَتَهَا وَهُدَاهَا وَأَعُوذُ بِكَ مِنْ شَرِّ مَا فِيهَا وَشَرِّ مَا بَعْدَهَا

Amsaynaa wa amsal mulku lillahi rabbil alameen. Allahummah innee as aluka khayra aadhal yawmi, fathaha, wa nasraha, wa nuraha, wa barakataha, wa hudaha, wa audhu bika min sharri maa feeha wa sharri maa b`adaha

The evening has come to me and the whole universe belongs to Allah who is The Lord of the worlds. O Allah, I ask of you the good of the night, it's success and aid and its nur (celestial light) and barakaat (blessings) and seek hidayat (guidance) and refuge from the evil of this night and the evil that is to come later.

Supplication Before Going to Bed

بِاسْمِكَ اللَّهُمَّ أَمُوتُ وَأَحْيَا

Bismika Allaahumma amootu wa ahyaa.
In Your name, O Allah, I die and I live.
Or:

اللَّهُمَّ أَسْلَمْتُ نَفْسِي إِلَيْكَ، وَفَوَّضْتُ أَمْرِي إِلَيْكَ، وَوَجَّهْتُ وَجْهِي إِلَيْكَ، وَأَلْجَأْتُ ظَهْرِي إِلَيْكَ، رَغْبَةً وَرَهْبَةً إِلَيْكَ، لَا مَلْجَأَ وَلَّا مَنْجَا مِنْكَ إِلَّا إِلَيْكَ، آمَنْتُ بِكِتَابِكَ الَّذِي وَبِنَبِيِّكَ الَّذِي أَرْسَلْتَ

Allaahumma 'aslamtu nafsee 'ilayka, wa fawwadhtu 'amree 'ilayka, wa wajjahtu wajhee 'ilayka, wa 'alja'tu dhahree 'ilayka, raghbatan wa rahbatan 'ilayka, laa malja' wa laa manja minka 'illaa 'ilayka, 'aamantu bikitaabikal-lathee 'anzalta wa bi-nabiyyikal-lathee 'arsalta.

O Allah, I submit myself to You, entrust my affairs to You, turn my face to You, and lay myself down depending upon You, hoping in You and fearing You. There is no refuge, and no escape, except to You. I believe in Your Book (the Qur'an) that You revealed, and the Prophet whom You sent.

Reference:

"Before you go to bed perform ablutions as you would for prayer, then lie down on your right side and say (the above prayer). " The Prophet (SAW) said: *"Whoever says this and dies in his sleep, has died in a state of the natural monotheism (Fitrah)."* Al-Bukhari, cf. Al-Asqalani, Fathul-Bari 11/113, Muslim 4/2081.

بِاسْمِكَ رَبِّي وَضَعْتُ جَنْبِي، وَبِكَ أَرْفَعُهُ، فَإِنْ أَمْسَكْتَ نَفْسِي فَارْحَمْهَا، وَإِنْ أَرْسَلْتَهَا فَاحْفَظْهَا، بِمَا تَحْفَظُ بِهِ عِبَادَكَ الصَّالِحِينَ".

Bismika Rabbee, wadha'tu janbee, wa bika 'arfa'uhu. Fa'in 'amsakta nafsee, farhamhaa, wa 'in 'arsaltahaa fahfadh haa, bimaa tahfadhu bihi 'ibaadakas-saaliheen.

With Your Name my Lord, I lay myself down; and with Your Name I rise. And if my soul You take, have mercy on it, and if You send it back then protect it as You protect Your righteous slaves.

Reference:

"If any of you rises from his bed and later returns to it, let him dust off his bed with his waist garment three times and mention the Name of Allah, for he does not know what may have entered the bed after him. Al-Bukhari 1 1/ 126 and Muslim 4/2084.

What to say if you are afraid to go to sleep or feel lonely and depressed

أَعُوذُ بِكَلِمَاتِ اللهِ التَّامَّاتِ مِنْ غَضَبِهِ وَعِقَابِهِ، وَشَرِّ عِبَادِهِ، وَمِنْ هَمَزَاتِ الشَّيَاطِينِ وَأَنْ يَحْضُرُونِ

'A'oodhu bikalimaatil-laahit-taammaati min ghadabihi wa 'iqaabihi, wa sharri 'ibaadihi, wa min hamazaatish-shayaateeni wa 'an yahdhuroon.

I seek refuge in the Perfect Words of Allah from His anger and His punishment, from the evil of His slaves and from the taunts of devils and from their presence.

What to do if you have a bad dream or nightmare
- Spit to your left (three times).[1]
- Seek refuge in Allah from the Devil and from the evil of what you have seen (three times).
- Do not speak about it to anyone
- Turn over on your other side when you wake up

الْحَمْدُ للهِ الَّذِي أَحْيَانَا بَعْدَ مَا أَمَاتَنَا وَإِلَيْهِ النُّشُورُ

Alhamdu lillaahil-ladhee 'ahyaanaa ba'da maa 'amaatanaa wa'ilayhin-nushoor.

29

Praise is to Allah Who gives us life after He has caused us to die and to Him is the return

What to say when leaving home

بِسْمِ اللهِ، تَوَكَّلْتُ عَلَى اللهِ، وَلَا حَوْلَ وَلَا قُوَّةَ إِلَّا بِاللهِ

Bismillaahi, tawakkaltu 'alallaahi, wa laa hawla wa laa quwwata ' illaa billaah.

In the Name of Allah, I have placed my trust in Allah, there is no might and no power except by Allah.

What to say when entering the home

بِسْمِ اللهِ وَلَجْنَا، وَ بِسْمِ اللهِ خَرَجْنَا، وَعَلَى رَبِّنَا تَوَكَّلْنَا

Bismillaahi walajnaa, wa bismillaahi kharajnaa, wa 'alaa Rabbinaa tawakkalnaa

In the Name of Allah we enter, in the Name of Allah we leave, and upon our Lord we depend (then say As-Salaamu 'Alaykum to those present).

Invocation for leaving the mosque

بِسْمِ اللهِ، وَالصَّلَاةُ وَالسَّلَامُ عَلَى رَسُولِ اللهِ، اللَّهُمَّ إِنِّي أَسْأَلُكَ مِنْ فَضْلِكَ

Bismillaahi wassalaatu wassalaamu 'alaa Rasoolillaahi, Allaahumma 'innee as aluka min fadhlika

In the Name of Allah, and peace and blessings be upon the Messenger of Allah. O Allah, I ask for Your favor.

Upon entering the Mosque

أَعوذُ بِاللهِ العَظيمِ وَبِوَجْهِهِ الكَرِيمِ وَسُلْطانِه القَديمِ مِنَ الشّيْطانِ الرَّجيم (بِسْمِ الله، وَالصَّلاةُ وَالسَّلامُ عَلى رَسولِ الله)،اللّهُمَّ افتَحْ لي أَبْوابَ رَحْمَتِك

'A'oodhu billaahil-'Adheem, wa bi-Wajhihil-Kareem, wa Sultaanihil-qadeem, minash-Shaytaanir-rajeem. (Bismillaahi, wassalaatu wassalaamu 'alaa Rasoolillaahi). Allaahumma ftah lee 'abwaaba rahmatika.

I seek refuge in Almighty Allah, by His Noble Face, by His primordial power, from Satan the outcast.[1] [In the Name of Allah, and blessings.] [And peace be upon the Messenger of Allah.] O Allah, open before me the doors of Your mercy.

Invocation against an enemy

اللَّهُمَّ مُنْزِلَ الْكِتَابِ سَرِيعَ الْحِسَابِ، اللَّهُمَّ اهْزِمِ الأَحْزَابَ، اللَّهُمَّ اهْزِمْهُمْ وَزَلْزِلْهُمْ

Allaahumma munzilal-kitaabi, saree 'al-hisaabi, Allahumma ihzimil-'ahzaaba, Allaahumma ihzimhum wa zalzilhum.

Allah, Revealer of the Book, Swift to account, defeat the groups (of disbelievers). O Allah, defeat them and shake them.

How to seek Allah's protection for children

The Prophet (SAW) used to seek Allah's protection for Al-Hasan and Al-Husain by saying:

أَعوذُ بِكَلِماتِ اللّهِ التّامّاتِ مِنْ شَرِّ ما خَلَق

A`ūdhu bikalimāti 'llāhit-tāmmāti min sharri mā khalaq
I seek refuge in the Perfect Words of Allah from the evil of what He has created.

'U'eedhukumaa bikalimaatil-laahit-taammati min kulli shaytaanin wa haammatin, wa min kulli 'aynin laammatin.

I seek protection for you in the Perfect Words of Allah from every devil and every beast , and from every envious blameworthy eye.

Invocation for when it rains

اللّهُمَّ صَيِّباً نافِعاً

Allaahumma sayyiban naafi'an

O Allah , (bring) beneficial rain clouds

Invocations before eating

When anyone of you begins eating, say:

"بِسْمِ اللَّهِ" . (بِسْمِ اللَّهِ في أَوَّلِهِ وَآخِرِهِ)

Bismillaah.

With the name of Allah.

And if you forget then, when you remember, say:

Bismillaahifee 'awwalihi wa 'aakhirihi.
With the Name of Allah, in the beginning and in the end.

Invocations after eating

الْحَمْدُ لِلَّهِ الَّذي أَطْعَمَني هـذا وَرَزَقَنيهِ مِنْ غَيْرِ حَوْلٍ مِنّي وَلا قُوَّةٍ

Alhamdu lillaahil-ladhee 'at'amanee haadha, wa razaqaneehi, min ghayri hawlin minnee wa laa quwwatin.
Praise is to Allah Who has given me this food and sustained me with it though I was unable to doit and powerless.

Invocation for traveling

اللَّهُ أَكْبَرُ، اللَّهُ أَكْبَرُ، اللَّهُ أَكْبَرُ، ﴿سُبْحانَ الَّذي سَخَّرَ لَنا هـذا وَما كُنَّا لَهُ مُقْرِنينَ * وَإِنَّا إِلى رَبِّنا لَمُنْقَلِبُونَ﴾ اللَّهُمَّ إِنّا نَسْأَلُكَ في سَفَرِنا هـذا الْبِرَّ وَالتَّقْوَى، وَمِنَ الْعَمَلِ ما تَرْضَى، اللَّهُمَّ هَوِّنْ عَلَيْنا سَفَرَنا هـذا وَاطْوِ عَنَّا بُعْدَهُ، اللَّهُمَّ أَنْتَ الصَّاحِبُ في السَّفَرِ، وَالْخَليفَةُ في الْأَهْلِ، اللَّهُمَّ إِنّي أَعُوذُ بِكَ مِنْ وَعْثاءِ السَّفَرِ، وَكَآبَةِ الْمَنْظَرِ، وَسُوءِ الْمُنْقَلَبِ في الْمالِ وَالْأَهْلِ

Allaahu 'Akbar, Allaahu 'Akbar, Allaahu 'Akbar, Subhaanal-ladhee sakhkhara lanaa hadhaa wa maa kunnaa lahu muqrineen. Wa innaa ilaa Rabbinaa lamunqaliboon. Allaahumma innaa nas'aluka fee safarinaa

haadhal-birrawattaqwaa, waminal-'amalimaa tardhaa, Allaahumma hawwin 'alaynaa safaranaa haadhaa watwi 'annaa bu'dahu, Allaahumma 'Antas-saahibu fis-safari, walkhaleefatu fil-'ahli, Allaahumma 'innee 'a'oodhu bika min wa'thaa'is-safari, wa ka'aabati-mandhari, wa soo'il-munqalabi fil-maaliwal'ahli.

Allah is the Most Great. Allah is the Most Great. Allah is the Most Great. Glory is to Him Who has provided this for us though we could never have had it by our efforts. Surely, unto our Lord we are returning. O Allah, we ask You on this our journey for goodness and piety, and for works that are pleasing to You. O Allah, lighten this journey for us and make its distance easy for us. O Allah, You are our Companion on the road and the One in Whose care we leave our family. O Allah, I seek refuge in You from this journey's hardships, and from the wicked sights in store and from finding our family and property in misfortune upon returning.

Upon returning recite the same again adding:

وإذا رَجَعَ قَالَهُنَّ وَزَادَ فِيهِنَّ: "آيِبُونَ، تائِبُونَ، عَابِدُونَ، لِرَبِّنَا حَامِدُونَ

'Aa'iboona, taa'iboona, 'aabidoona, Lirabbinaa haamidoon.

We return repentant to our Lord, worshipping our Lord, and praising our Lord.

The traveler's invocation for the ones he leaves behind

أَسْتَوْدِعُكُمُ اللهَ الَّذِي لا تَضِيعُ وَدائِعُه

'Astawdi'ukumul-laahal-ladhee laa tadhee'u wadaa'i'uhu.
I leave you in the care of Allah, as nothing is lost that is in His care.

Rabbanas (Prayers starting with "Our Lord") from the Qur'an

رَبَّنَا تَقَبَّلْ مِنَّا إِنَّكَ أَنْتَ السَّمِيعُ العَلِيمُ

Rabbana taqabbal minnaa innaka Antas Samee'ul Aleem
"Our Lord, accept [this] from us. Indeed You are the Hearing,
the Knowing."
– 2:127 –

رَبَّنَا وَاجْعَلْنَا مُسْلِمَيْنِ لَكَ وَمِن ذُرِّيَّتِنَا أُمَّةً مُّسْلِمَةً لَّكَ وَأَرِنَا مَنَاسِكَنَا وَتُبْ
عَلَيْنَا إِنَّكَ أَنتَ التَّوَّابُ الرَّحِيمُ

Rabbana waj'alnaa muslimaini laka wa min zurriyyatinaaa
ummatam muslimatal laka wa arinaa manaasikanaa wa
tub 'alainaa innaka antat Tawwaabur Raheem
"Our Lord, and make us Muslims [in submission] to You and
from our descendants a Muslim nation [in submission] to You.
And show us our rites [of worship] and accept our repentance.
Indeed, You are the Accepting of Repentance, the Merciful."
– 2:128 –

رَبَّنَا آتِنَا فِي الدُّنْيَا حَسَنَةً وَفِي الآخِرَةِ حَسَنَةً وَقِنَا عَذَابَ النَّارِ

Rabbana atina fid dunyaa hasanatanw wa fil aakhirati
hasanatanw wa qinaa azaaban Naar

"Our Lord, give us in this world [that which is] good and in the
Hereafter [that which is] good and protect us from the
punishment of the Fire."

– 2:201 –

رَبَّنَا أَفْرِغْ عَلَيْنَا صَبْراً وَثَبِّتْ أَقْدَامَنَا وَانصُرْنَا عَلَى الْقَوْمِ الْكَافِرِينَ

Rabbana afrigh 'alainaa sabranw wa sabbit aqdaamanaa
wansurnaa 'alal qawmil kaafireen

"Our Lord, pour upon us patience and plant firmly our feet and
give us victory over the disbelieving people."

– 2:250 –

رَبَّنَا لاَ تُؤَاخِذْنَا إِن نَّسِينَا أَوْ أَخْطَأْنَا

Rabbana laa tu'aakhiznaaa in naseenaaa aw akhtaanaa

"Our Lord, do not impose blame upon us if we have forgotten or
erred."

– 2:286 –

رَبَّنَا وَلاَ تَحْمِلْ عَلَيْنَا إِصْرًا كَمَا حَمَلْتَهُۥ عَلَى الَّذِينَ مِن قَبْلِنَا

Rabbana wa laa tahmil-'alainaaa isran kamaa hamaltahoo
'alal-lazeena min qablinaa

"Our Lord, and lay not upon us a burden like that which You laid upon those before us."

– 2:286 –

لَنَا وَارْحَمْنَا أَنتَ مَوْلَانَا فَانصُرْنَا عَلَى الْقَوْمِ الْكَافِرِينَ

Rabbana wa laa tuhammilnaa maa laa taaqata lanaa bih;
wa'fu 'annaa waghfir lanaa warhamnaa; Anta mawlaanaa
fansurnaa 'alal qawmil kaafireen

"Our Lord, and burden us not with that which we have no ability to bear. And pardon us; and forgive us; and have mercy upon us. You are our protector, so give us victory over the disbelieving people."

– 2:286 –

رَبَّنَا لاَ تُزِغْ قُلُوبَنَا بَعْدَ إِذْ هَدَيْتَنَا وَهَبْ لَنَا مِن لَّدُنكَ رَحْمَةً إِنَّكَ أَنتَ الْوَهَّابُ

Rabbana laa tuzigh quloobanaa ba'da iz hadaitanaa wa hab
lanaa mil ladunka rahmah; innaka antal Wahhaab

"Our Lord, let not our hearts deviate after You have guided us and grant us from Yourself mercy. Indeed, You are the Bestower."

– 3:8 –

رَبَّنَا إِنَّكَ جَامِعُ النَّاسِ لِيَوْمٍ لاَّ رَيْبَ فِيهِ إِنَّ اللهَ لاَ يُخْلِفُ الْمِيعَادَ

Rabbana innaka jami'unnasi li-Yawmil la raiba fi innallaha la yukhliful mi'aad

"Our Lord, surely You will gather the people for a Day about which there is no doubt. Indeed, Allah does not fail in His promise."

– 3:9 –

رَبَّنَا إِنَّنَا آمَنَّا فَاغْفِرْ لَنَا ذُنُوبَنَا وَقِنَا عَذَابَ النَّارِ

Rabbanaaa innanaaa aamannaa faghfir lanaa zunoobanaa wa qinaa 'azaaban Naar

"Our Lord, indeed we have believed, so forgive us our sins and protect us from the punishment of the Fire"

– 3:16 –

رَبَّنَا ءَامَنَّا بِمَا أَنزَلْتَ وَٱتَّبَعْنَا ٱلرَّسُولَ فَٱكْتُبْنَا مَعَ ٱلشَّٰهِدِينَ

Rabbanaaa aamannaa bimaaa anzalta wattaba'nar Rasoola faktubnaa ma'ash shaahideen

"Our Lord, we have believed in what You revealed and have followed the messenger [i.e., Jesus], so register us among the witnesses [to truth]."

– 3:53 –

38

رَبَّنَا اغْفِرْ لَنَا ذُنُوبَنَا وَإِسْرَافَنَا فِي أَمْرِنَا وَثَبِّتْ أَقْدَامَنَا وانصُرْنَا عَلَى الْقَوْمِ الْكَافِرِينَ ۞

Rabbanagh fir lanaa zunoobanaa wa israafanaa feee amirnaa wa sabbit aqdaamanaa wansurnaa 'alal qawmil kaafireen

"Our Lord, forgive us our sins and the excess [committed] in our affairs and plant firmly our feet and give us victory over the disbelieving people."

– 3:147 –

رَبَّنَا مَا خَلَقْتَ هذا بَاطِلاً سُبْحَانَكَ فَقِنَا عَذَابَ النَّارِ

Rabbanaa maa khalaqta haaza baatilan Subhaanaka faqinaa 'azaaban Naar

"Our Lord, You did not create this aimlessly; exalted are You [above such a thing]; then protect us from the punishment of the Fire."

– 3:191 –

رَبَّنَا إِنَّكَ مَن تُدْخِلِ النَّارَ فَقَدْ أَخْزَيْتَهُ ۗ وَمَا لِلظَّالِمِينَ مِنْ أَنصَارٍ

Rabbana innaka man tudkhilin Naara faqad akhzai tahoo wa maa lizzaalimeena min ansaar

"Our Lord, indeed whoever You admit to the Fire – You have

39

disgraced him, and for the wrongdoers there are no helpers."
– 3:192 –

رَبَّنَا إِنَّنَا سَمِعْنَا مُنَادِيًا يُنَادِي لِلْإِيمَانِ أَنْ آمِنُوا بِرَبِّكُمْ فَآمَنَّا

*Rabbanaaa innanaa sami'naa munaadiyai yunaadee lil
eemaani an aaminoo bi Rabbikum fa aamannaa*

"Our Lord, indeed we have heard a caller, calling to faith,
[saying], 'Believe in your Lord,' and we have believed."
– 3:193 –

رَبَّنَا فَاغْفِرْ لَنَا ذُنُوبَنَا وَكَفِّرْ عَنَّا سَيِّئَاتِنَا وَتَوَفَّنَا مَعَ الْأَبْرَارِ

*Rabbanaa faghfir lanaa zunoobanaa wa kaffir 'annaa saiyi
aatina wa tawaffanaa ma'al abraar*

"Our Lord, so forgive us our sins and remove from us our
misdeeds and cause us to die among the righteous."
– 3:193 –

رَبَّنَا وَآتِنَا مَا وَعَدْتَّنَا عَلَى رُسُلِكَ وَلَا تُخْزِنَا يَوْمَ الْقِيَامَةِ إِنَّكَ لَا تُخْلِفُ الْمِيعَا
د

*Rabbana wa 'atina ma wa'adtana 'ala rusulika wa la
tukhzina yawmal- Qiyamah innaka la tukhliful mi'aad*

"Our Lord, and grant us what You promised us through Your
messengers and do not disgrace us on the Day of Resurrection.

Indeed, You do not fail in [Your] promise."

– 3:194 –

رَبَّنَا آمَنَّا فَاكْتُبْنَا مَعَ الشَّاهِدِينَ

Rabbana aamana faktubna ma' ash-shahideen

"Our Lord, we have believed, so register us among the witnesses."

– 5:83 –

رَبَّنَا أَنزِلْ عَلَيْنَا مَآئِدَةً مِّنَ السَّمَاءِ تَكُونُ لَنَا عِيداً لِّأَوَّلِنَا وَآخِرِنَا وَآيَةً مِّنكَ وَارْزُقْنَا وَأَنتَ خَيْرُ الرَّازِقِينَ

Rabbana anzil 'alaina ma'idatam minas-Samai takunu lana 'idal li-awwa-lina wa aakhirna wa ayatam-minka war-zuqna wa anta Khayrul-Raziqeen

"O Allah, our Lord, send down to us a table [spread with food] from the heaven to be for us a festival for the first of us and the last of us and a sign from You. And provide for us, and You are the best of providers."

– 5:114 –

رَبَّنَا ظَلَمْنَا أَنفُسَنَا وَإِن لَّمْ تَغْفِرْ لَنَا وَتَرْحَمْنَا لَنَكُونَنَّ مِنَ الْخَاسِرِينَ

Rabbana zalamna anfusina wa il lam taghfir lana wa tarhamna lanakoonanna minal khaasireen

"Our Lord, we have wronged ourselves, and if You do not

41

forgive us and have mercy upon us, we will surely be among the losers."

– 7:23 –

رَبَّنَا لَا تَجْعَلْنَا مَعَ الْقَوْمِ الظَّالِمِينَ

Rabbana la taj'alna ma'al qawwmi-dhalimeen

"Our Lord, do not place us with the wrongdoing people."

– 7:47 –

رَبَّنَا افْتَحْ بَيْنَنَا وَبَيْنَ قَوْمِنَا بِالْحَقِّ وَأَنتَ خَيْرُ الْفَاتِحِينَ

Rabbanaf-tah bainana wa baina qawmina bil haqqi wa anta Khairul Fatiheen

"Our Lord, decide between us and our people in truth, and You are the best of those who give decision."

– 7:89 –

رَبَّنَا أَفْرِغْ عَلَيْنَا صَبْرًا وَتَوَفَّنَا مُسْلِمِينَ

Rabbana afrigh 'alaina sabraw wa tawaffana Muslimeen

"Our Lord, pour upon us patience and let us die as Muslims [in submission to You]."

– 7:126 –

رَبَّنَا لَا تَجْعَلْنَا فِتْنَةً لِّلْقَوْمِ الظَّالِمِينَ ؛ وَنَجِّنَا بِرَحْمَتِكَ مِنَ الْقَوْمِ الْكَافِرِينَ

85. Rabbana la taj'alna fitnatal lil-qawmidh-Dhalimeen ; 86. wa najjina bi- Rahmatika minal qawmil kafireen
"Our Lord, make us not [objects of] trial for the wrongdoing people. And save us by Your mercy from the disbelieving people."
– 10:85-86 –

رَبَّنَا إِنَّكَ تَعْلَمُ مَا نُخْفِي وَمَا نُعْلِنُ وَمَا يَخْفَى عَلَى مِن شَيْءٍ فِي الأَرْضِ وَلاَ فِي السَّمَاء

Rabbanaa innaka ta'lamu maa nukhfee wa maa nu'lin; wa maa yakhfaa 'alal laahi min shai'in fil ardi wa laa fis samaaa
"Our Lord, indeed You know what we conceal and what we declare, and nothing is hidden from Allah on the earth or in the heaven."
– 14:38 –

رَبِّ اجْعَلْنِي مُقِيمَ الصَّلَاةِ وَمِنْ ذُرِّيَّتِي رَبَّنَا وَتَقَبَّلْ دُعَاءِ

Rabbij 'alnee muqeemas Salaati wa min zurriyyatee Rabbanaa wa taqabbal du'aaa
"My Lord, make me an establisher of prayer, and [many] from my descendants. Our Lord, and accept my supplication."
– 14:40 –

رَبَّنَا اغْفِرْ لِي وَلِوَالِدَيَّ وَلِلْمُؤْمِنِينَ يَوْمَ يَقُومُ الْحِسَابُ

Rabbanagh fir lee wa liwaalidaiya wa lilmu'mineena
Yawma yaqoomul hisaab

"Our Lord, forgive me and my parents and the believers the Day
the account is established."

– 14:41 –

رَبَّنَا آتِنَا مِن لَّدُنكَ رَحْمَةً وَهَيِّئْ لَنَا مِنْ أَمْرِنَا رَشَدًا

Rabbana 'atina mil-ladunka Rahmataw wa haiyi lana min
amrina rashada

"Our Lord, grant us from Yourself mercy and prepare for us
from our affair right guidance."

– 18:10 –

رَبَّنَا إِنَّنَا نَخَافُ أَن يَفْرُطَ عَلَيْنَا أَوْ أَن يَطْغَى

Rabbana innana nakhafu ai-yafruta 'alaina aw any-yatgha

"Our Lord, indeed we are afraid that he will hasten
[punishment] against us or that he will transgress."

– 20:45 –

رَبَّنَا آمَنَّا فَاغْفِرْ لَنَا وَارْحَمْنَا وَأَنتَ خَيْرُ الرَّاحِمِينَ

Rabbana amanna faghfir lana warhamna wa anta khairur
Rahimiin

"Our Lord, we have believed, so forgive us and have mercy

44

upon us, and You are the best of the merciful."

– 23:109 –

رَبَّنَا اصْرِفْ عَنَّا عَذَابَ جَهَنَّمَ إِنَّ عَذَابَهَا كَانَ غَرَامًا إِنَّهَا سَاءتْ مُسْتَقَرًّا وَمُقَامًا

65. Rabbanas-rif 'anna 'adhaba jahannama inna 'adhabaha kana gharama 66. innaha sa'at musta-qarranw wa muqama

"Our Lord, avert from us the punishment of Hell. Indeed, its punishment is ever adhering; Indeed, it is evil as a settlement and residence."

– 25:65-66 –

رَبَّنَا هَبْ لَنَا مِنْ أَزْوَاجِنَا وَذُرِّيَّاتِنَا قُرَّةَ أَعْيُنٍ وَاجْعَلْنَا لِلْمُتَّقِينَ إِمَامًا

Rabbana Hablana min azwaajina wadhurriy-yatina, qurrata 'ayioni wa-jalna lil-muttaqeena Imaama

"Our Lord, grant us from among our wives and offspring comfort to our eyes and make us a leader [i.e., example] for the righteous."

– 25:74 –

رَبَّنَا لَغَفُورٌ شَكُورٌ

Rabbana la Ghafurun shakur
"Our Lord is Forgiving and Appreciative"
– 35:34 –

رَبَّنَا وَسِعْتَ كُلَّ شَيْءٍ رَّحْمَةً وَعِلْمًا فَاغْفِرْ لِلَّذِينَ تَابُوا وَاتَّبَعُوا سَبِيلَكَ وَقِهِمْ عَذَابَ الْجَحِيمِ

Rabbana wasi'ta kulla sha'ir Rahmatanw wa 'ilman faghfir lilladhina tabu wattaba'u sabilaka waqihim 'adhabal-Jahiim
"Our Lord, You have encompassed all things in mercy and knowledge, so forgive those who have repented and followed Your way and protect them from the punishment of Hellfire."
– 40:7 –

رَبَّنَا وَأَدْخِلْهُمْ جَنَّاتِ عَدْنٍ الَّتِي وَعَدتَّهُمْ وَمَن صَلَحَ مِنْ آبَائِهِمْ وَأَزْوَاجِهِمْ وَذُرِّيَّاتِهِمْ إِنَّكَ أَنتَ الْعَزِيزُ الْحَكِيمُ وَقِهِمُ السَّيِّئَاتِ وَمَن تَقِ السَّيِّئَاتِ يَوْمَئِذٍ فَقَدْ رَحِمْتَهُ وَذَلِكَ هُوَ الْفَوْزُ الْعَظِيمُ

8. Rabbana wa adhkhilhum Jannati 'adninil-lati wa'attahum wa man salaha min aba'ihim wa azwajihim wa dhuriyyatihim innaka antal 'Azizul-Hakim, 9. waqihimus saiyi'at wa man taqis-saiyi'ati yawma'idhin faqad rahimatahu wa dhalika huwal fawzul-'Adheem

46

"Our Lord, and admit them to gardens of perpetual residence which You have promised them and whoever was righteous among their forefathers, their spouses and their offspring. Indeed, it is You who is the Exalted in Might, the Wise. And protect them from the evil consequences [of their deeds]. And he whom You protect from evil consequences that Day – You will have given him mercy. And that is the great attainment."
– 40:8-9 –

رَبَّنَا اغْفِرْ لَنَا وَلِإِخْوَانِنَا الَّذِينَ سَبَقُونَا بِالْإِيمَانِ وَلَا تَجْعَلْ فِي قُلُوبِنَا غِلًّا لِلَّذِينَ آمَنُوا

Rabbana-ghfir lana wa li 'ikhwani nalladhina sabaquna bil imani wa la taj'al fi qulubina ghillal-lilladhina amanu
"Our Lord, forgive us and our brothers who preceded us in faith and put not in our hearts [any] resentment toward those who have believed."
– 59:10 –

رَبَّنَا إِنَّكَ رَؤُوفٌ رَّحِيمٌ

Rabbana innaka Ra'ufur Rahim

"Our Lord, indeed You are Kind and Merciful."

– 59:10 –

رَبَّنَا عَلَيْكَ تَوَكَّلْنَا وَإِلَيْكَ أَنَبْنَا وَإِلَيْكَ الْمَصِيرُ

Rabbana 'alaika tawakkalna wa-ilaika anabna wa-ilaikal masir

"Our Lord, upon You we have relied, and to You we have returned, and to You is the destination."

– 60:4 –

رَبَّنَا لَا تَجْعَلْنَا فِتْنَةً لِّلَّذِينَ كَفَرُوا وَاغْفِرْ لَنَا رَبَّنَا إِنَّكَ أَنتَ الْعَزِيزُ الْحَكِيمُ

Rabbana la taj'alna fitnatal lilladhina kafaru waghfir lana Rabbana innaka antal 'Azeezul-Hakeem

"Our Lord, make us not [objects of] torment for the disbelievers and forgive us, our Lord. Indeed, it is You who is the Exalted in Might, the Wise."

– 60:5 –

رَبَّنَا أَتْمِمْ لَنَا نُورَنَا وَاغْفِرْ لَنَا إِنَّكَ عَلَى كُلِّ شَيْءٍ قَدِيرٌ

Rabbana atmim lana nurana waighfir lana innaka 'ala kulli shai-in qadir

"Our Lord, perfect for us our light and forgive us. Indeed, You are over all things competent."

– 66:8 –

About Masjid Mubarak

Masjid Mubarak (Nigerian-American Islamic Mission - NAIM) is located in Newark, New Jersey's largest city. The Masjid's mission is to offer Muslims a place to congregate to worship and to learn about the teachings of Islam. The Masjid seeks to inculcate in Muslims Islamic teachings and the brotherhood of mankind. Programs such as weekly Tafsir — Quran study/exegesis sessions, (which are also accessible via teleconference), and lectures are held to educate Muslims of the community, and to aid them in their spiritual development.

The Masjid offers an impressive Arabic and Islamic studies program for children and adults, taught by knowledgeable scholars. It also serves as an Islamic Cultural center where Muslims hold various events such as Naming ceremonies (Aqeeqah) and Weddings. The Masjid also hosts an active Muslim Youth program that seeks to promote brotherhood and Islamic culture and learning amongst Muslim youth of the community. The Masjid also engages in various community outreach services, including a Food Pantry program that seeks to address the issue of food insecurity in its local community.

Please support the work of the Masjid by donating through its website at **www.naimnj.org**, or directly through Zelle: *finance@naimnj.org*

Made in the USA
Middletown, DE
11 April 2021